WHAT YOUR MOTHER SHOULD'VE TOLD YOU

WHAT YOUR MOTHER SHOULD'VE TOLD YOU

and nobody else will

NATALIE REILLY

The Robson Press

This edition published in Great Britain in 2013 by
The Robson Press (an imprint of Biteback Publishing Ltd)
Westminster Tower
3 Albert Embankment
London SE1 7SP
Copyright © Natalie Reilly 2012

First published by Allen & Unwin, Sydney, Australia.

ISBN 978-1-84954-620-1

10 9 8 7 6 5 4 3 2 1

A CIP catalogue record for this book is available from the British Library.

Set in Bodoni

Printed and bound in Great Britain by
CPI Group (UK) Ltd, Croydon CR0 4YY

Contents

Introduction

A movie critic once wrote the reason he chose his occupation was not because he was an expert on movies but because he had a passion for them not shared by many other people.

It's the same for me with giving advice. It may not always have been solicited, but my passion for giving it has never waned. I consider it a Reilly family gift – handed down from generation to generation.

My grandfather once approached a successful football player to tell him he would be better off playing Rugby League. My father, too, was famous for doling out the occasional hard truth – for which his justification was always, 'If I don't tell you, nobody else will.'

But if that was Dad's motto, my mum's was: 'Before you judge someone, walk a mile in their shoes.' And luckily some of Mum's compassion moderated the more, some might say, 'tough love' tendencies of my compulsive advising.

By my 20s, I found myself the Agony Aunt not just for my friends, but for my sister's friends, and their friends – and so on. My boss called me 'Miss Manners' with only a hint of irony. And for that, I sent her a thank you note.

I knew things had reached a whole new level when a person I'd just met asked for career advice. 'Well, Sally—' I began. 'It's Sophie,' she said, 'but go on.'

And so, when the opportunity arose to write a book about all the things people should know these days, I jumped at it. My aim is to give you up-to-date information on everything from modern manners to lessons on life.

These opinions are not off the top of my head, but have been painstakingly researched, for which I'd like to thank Google and the myriad lessons in my own life, which I've had to learn the hard way.

Throughout this book you may notice a few recurring themes, like the fact that when people behave badly, it's usually because they're scared; and that being the bigger bloke is often its own reward. These are guidelines I try to live by (albeit imperfectly), and you should find they'll see you through almost every situation.

Other than that, *my advice* is to cherry-pick what works for you. Some of what I have to say might be a little hard to swallow, but advice without truth is merely trite. And while truthful advice runs the risk of offending, it's a risk, dear reader, I'm willing to take. Because, as my father said, if I don't tell you ...

Life lessons

How to be happy

We're always encouraged to do what makes us happy, but the catch is that what we think will make us happy and what actually makes us happy are often wildly contradictory. Besides which, a little bit of pessimism is actually good for you – it's unrealistic to expect to be happy all the time.

If you've been down in the dumps for months now, or you've lost a loved one or your job, or you've broken up with someone, then I'm happy to admit that these meagre 400-or-so words are not about to turn you around – you've been through the ringer so be kind to yourself and don't hesitate to see a professional.

But, if your moods generally err on the side of blue it's time to buck up! Because you can change – if you want to.

Rule number one: you may feel like isolating but it's not the answer. You can enjoy socialising, just pick people you can be your curmudgeonly self around. The more you talk through what's bothering you, the quicker you'll recover. As Elton sang, that's what friends are for.

Speaking of: listen to music. And while you're listening to it, walk. You don't have to download 'Walking on

Sunshine' but you don't have to indulge in Leonard Cohen either. Pick a few songs that are uplifting and walk it out. Research shows that exercise lifts your mood. And listening to music you love does too, so imagine what combining them will do for you!

Marty Seligman, the godfather of positive psychology, recommends this and so do I: a 'grateful journal'. At the moment, you're probably thinking 'What do I have to be grateful for?' Well, this is about realigning your brain to focus on the positive. Once you get used to recording five good things that happened to you at the end of every day (no matter how small), your brain will slowly gravitate towards the positive rather than the negative.

Finally, get your mind off yourself. This is not just tough love; research proves this is the key to happiness. Go be of service to friends and family. If you don't have either, then help an old person cross the road. Stand up for someone on the bus. Give change to the Salvation Army. Smile.

The pleasant by-product of this method is a rise in self-esteem. And once you start to feel like you're worth something you'll find happiness – because it's in you, I promise, and it's busting to come out.

How to make friends

Making friends as a grown-up can be challenging – especially if you're a little on the introverted side. But it's not impossible.

I know social-networking sites are the scourge of existence for some, but they also happen to be the easiest way to set up a friendship without appearing as if you, you know, desire a romantic interlude.

So, if you're out and you're introduced to someone you want to be friends with, hop on Facebook or Twitter. And do it straight away – the games that apply in romance do not work in friendship, where the majority of people are already a little on the shy side.

If you don't get out much, Facebook is still a useful tool. If you like what someone has said on your friend's wall, there is no reason why you can't cross-pollinate. There are also hundreds of home-made blogs literally begging to be commented on. And it's surprisingly easy to develop a friendship from one kind remark.

Of course, you can join clubs, groups and sports teams and initiate the after-work drinks with potential office buddies.

But with any of these methods, it's hard to make friends if you don't first have your attitude aligned to friend-making. Look, I know how that sounds, so let's just say that the advice your mother gave you still stands: smile, ask questions, don't fold your arms.

If you're still feeling reticent, remember it's not what you say that matters but the fact that you started a conversation in the first place – because, as the all-powerful Oprah says: in the end, everyone just wants to be heard.

How to survive a setback

Maybe you missed out on that job you were going for; maybe you didn't get the house – or the loan for the house. Or, maybe it's personal – maybe something you wanted to go in a certain way turned out a mess. Maybe someone close to you let you down.

No matter the origin, it's difficult to dust yourself off and try, try, try again when you feel like you've been, well, punched in the guts.

So, don't. It's fine to take some time and grieve over the lost position, the failed pitch, the one that got away. You can be sad because it is sad, but you don't have to sink into self-pity. And, yes, there is a difference. Sad says, 'Oh well.' Self-pity says, 'Nothing good ever happens to me,' and it works like quicksand: you sink in a flash and it's very hard to climb out again.

This is where friends can come in, to sit with you and to gently steer you back to reality when those statements crop up in your head. So, make sure you surround yourself with friends. And the right friends, too – nobody needs hollow platitudes about doors closing and windows opening.

The next thing you can do is indulge yourself. Go out for a nice meal, go get that massage, go buy those shoes. Maybe someone wasn't respectful of your feelings, but that doesn't mean you're undeserving of respect. You can indulge yourself in small ways, too. Take time out if you can, just to relax.

Remind yourself of your own strengths. The easiest way to do this is ... to use them. If you're a good cook, then start cooking. If you're good at tennis, go hire out a court.

Then, when you're feeling strong enough, make a frank assessment of the situation. This only comes with hindsight, when you no longer feel so fragile you need to hide your mistakes from yourself, so there's no point rushing it. But when you're up to it, ask yourself: What was my part in this? Is there anything I could have done differently? That way, if it ever happens again, you'll know what to avoid. Alternatively, you will accept that this sort of thing can happen to anyone.

And while I'm not about to give you the 'door closing/ window opening' speech I can say that as you're still alive (and reading this) you're already on your way out – slowly, yes, but surely.

How to appear smarter

In this age of sound bites and celebrities, it is comforting to know that intelligence is still considered something of a status symbol.

But knowledge alone will not produce mass approval, so avoid shouting out non sequiturs about WikiLeaks or the history of the railroad at your next dinner party.

Knowledge is like pasta: on its own it can be terribly bland but mix it up with a bit of sauce and it gains instant appeal. Look at that Stephen Fry show *QI* – those comedians rarely sound like Einstein but because they couch their comments in humour, it flies.

So, even if you only know a modicum of detail about Julian Assange's methodology, add a dollop of wit and you'll be fine. If you have no idea about a topic, listen to those who do. This is half of appearing intelligent – paying attention to what people say.

The saying 'Better to remain silent and be thought a fool than to speak out and remove all doubt' is a useful one in an emergency. But ideally you should hover somewhere in between.

This means asking questions – the Socratic method, which roughly translates as 'And then what happened?' If you're asking questions it means you're interested, and if you're interested in this intelligent subject, then you must understand it on some level.

Even if you don't, asking questions means you'll be thought of as charming, which is certainly equal to if not more highly valued than smarts.

Carpe diem, my friends.

How to say no

We all have to do things we don't want to, but if you routinely end up in situations that you'd rather avoid, or in which you feel uncomfortable or taken for granted, it's time to start using the N word.

Doing things that only satisfy the needs of others damages your self-esteem, and being self-sacrificial, while it can feel rewarding in the short term, has the potential to turn into seething resentment. And then all those demanding friends, colleagues, lovers and relatives end up asking, 'What happened? You used to be nice!'

The thing is, you are nice. Nice people can set boundaries too. If you have to, tell yourself out loud: 'It's okay to say no to a road trip with the in-laws/ lending money to the boss/letting my friend camp on my floor for two weeks.'

This might sound strange if you've never done it before but your needs and wants are just as important as other people's. It takes practice. So, start small. Say no to the windscreen washer or telemarketer. Then say no to an acquaintance. Then a co-worker.

Focus on your needs when you say no. For instance, if that co-worker asks you to help her out with her work, think about the report you're supposed to finish today – and how you'll feel if you don't do it. Focus on how you'll feel when you have that friend asleep on your couch while you tiptoe around them, trying not to wake them while you get ready for work. It's not great, is it? Explain your reasons for not helping the person in a calm, empathetic way and stand your ground.

Now, work your way up to the person who scares you the most. It might be the boss. It could be your mum. But remember that saying no is a lot like quitting smoking: it's hard now, but not quitting is harder. The sooner you start saying no, the easier it will be – for everyone.

How to handle yourself in an argument

It might be that someone has baited you. It might be that a dispassionate debate has turned a corner and lunged into personal territory. It might simply be a difference of opinion. But if someone is forcefully disagreeing with you, it can be hard in the heat of the moment to utter 'Agree to disagree!'

First, breathe. How important is this argument to you? Next, how important is it that this person sees your point of view? Now, the toughie: is this really about the subject? Or is there a possibility that the subject represents something deeper? For instance, does the fact that someone enjoys reading celebrity gossip mean, in your eyes, that they're shallow? And have you always wanted to call them shallow? It's all about motivations. And questions, lots of questions, wouldn't you agree?

So, after you've asked yourself these questions, calmly concede as many points of the other person's as you can manage. This has the effect of softening the force of their fury and will probably mean that they'll concede some of your points too. Letting someone know they have 'a point' on a small issue displays reason, thereby lending your own argument greater credibility.

It's usually after these two things have played out that the argument deflates and can be put away. At least until you see them again. And then you might have to ask yourself yet another couple of questions: Has arguing become a form of bonding? And if it has, is the feeling of winning worth the conflict? Do you really think you can change their beliefs by arguing?

I don't want to get into a scrape over this but it might be worth thinking about next time you want to go head to head.

How to speak in public

So, it's a wedding speech, or it's a work presentation or you've been called upon to 'say a few words' at a party. Perhaps you've noticed your stomach is now filled with a dozen butterflies.

Whatever it is, you don't need to picture the audience in their underwear to get through it. This is because the audience wants you to succeed. They want to be entertained or informed or moved and to this end they'll move with you, not because you're perfect but because – are you ready for this? – they're only human themselves.

In fact, as long as you have three main points, you'll be fine. Any more than this and people may tune out, any less, and it's not a speech, it's an outburst.

Some believe that speaking off the cuff makes for a more authentic, spontaneous delivery, but unless you're Barack Obama this is not recommended. So, rehearse those three main points because the more prepared you are, the less chance you have of being rattled.

And if you're speaking in front of a serious crowd then by all means, bring your notes. There is nothing wrong with bringing small cue cards to speeches, but make sure the occasion is grand enough to warrant it, i.e. not your kitchen.

But what if you stammer? What if you shake? What if you blush? What if you do all three? I'm telling you, from the top of this lectern, that none of these will matter. They can even be endearing – just be sure to own them. Saying 'Wow, I'm a bit nervous!' will actually make for a more relaxed atmosphere.

Anyway, if all else fails, remember that people only ever retain 20 per cent of what you tell them. If people are drinking, you can lower that number to 10 per cent. And if you've been drinking? Then mazel tov! You probably won't remember a thing.

How to budget like you mean it

If you're after a new bathroom or a new car or a quick jaunt to Barbados, then drawing up a budget is a straightforward and handy way to keep track of where all your money goes so you can save effectively.

Experts recommend doing a monthly budget but it's probably best to have your budget reflect your pay cycle, which might be fortnightly or weekly.

First, gather all your receipts and financial statements together. This will give you an idea of how much you're spending in any given month, fortnight, etc. Then, record your total income. It is at this point that you might want to break out the old Excel spreadsheet on your computer – it's great at minimising confusion (especially if maths isn't your strong suit).

Work out which expenses you absolutely have to pay, like mortgage, electricity, phone, credit card – these are your fixed expenses. Then, work out your variable expenses, also known as your 'fun money'. Groceries may or may not come under this umbrella so you might want to have a separate budget for food.

There are some financial experts who recommend withdrawing all your 'fun money' in one go and dealing in cash for everything until the next pay cycle. The advantage of this is you'll always know how much money you have left and you'll probably save a bundle on bank and EFTPOS fees.

The disadvantage is that if you're like me, if you see lots of money you think you're richer than you are and you might be tempted to spend more. Also, if somebody steals your wallet you're stuffed. It's a personal choice.

But back to your expenses: you know as well as I do that both variable and fixed should not exceed your income, or you'll be in debt.

There are some experts who recommend saving 20 per cent of your income, while others say 30 per cent, and still others, just 10 per cent. It's a wonderful idea to have your savings directly debited from each pay so you don't feel the pain of actually putting it away. Especially if it's 30 per cent.

Then again, it all depends on how quickly you want to get to Barbados, doesn't it?

How to not let money rule your life

Economics editor Ross Gittins wrote, 'Once a country reaches a reasonable level of affluence, it's not how much money it has so much as how well it uses what it's got.' And the same holds true for people.

But because money has intruded so far into our lives (even our personalities are now referred to as 'brands'), it feels sometimes that we can't separate our joy from our cash. And while being broke is no walk in the park, very few of us who worry about money are poverty-stricken.

It's easy to believe that if we were just rich enough money would cease to matter, but studies show the opposite is true.

The solution is not to penny-pinch (because you're still thinking about money) but to refocus your goals.

It sounds frightfully New Age-y but see if instead of *doing* things, you can start *being*. If you're *being* yourself, chances are you're around people who care about you – so top up your time with them. Not at a shopping centre, mind! But at each other's homes or the beach or a park.

Now, start giving it away. I know this is counter-intuitive but if you begin giving only a small amount to a charity, not only will this make you aware of how rich you are compared to, say, a kid in the Horn of Africa; you'll also begin to feel better about yourself. And when your self-esteem rises, you won't need so many material things to make you feel good. You'll also become used to a lower income, and you'll probably realise you can live on less.

Finally, you're doing it right now so chances are you enjoy it: read books. All that time taken up by buying and spending can just as easily be devoted to reading. And if you go to a library or a bookworm's home, you're sure to find a great supply – for free. Jackpot!

How to reduce your carbon footprint at home

One of the reasons it's not easy being green is because people like me feel we have to take drastic measures – like turning the backyard into a composting toilet – to really make a difference. But there are a few minor things you can do around the home to help save the planet – and save on your electricity bills in winter, too.

This is obvious, but watch how you shop. We're all avoiding plastic bags these days, of course, but food wastage is apparently a biggie.

Turn off as many of your appliances as you can at the power point. You can cut your household's carbon pollution by as much as 500 kilograms a year just by switching these off.

Use energy-efficient light bulbs. I know some of them take a little while to light up, but that's perfect when you've got to pee in the middle of the night and want to avoid being blinded, right?

Keep your heating (and cooling) system hovering at about 21 degrees. Ceiling insulation is highly recommended for trapping the heat. But if that's not in your house – or your budget – you can invest in draught blockers for your closed doors and thick curtains to pull across all your windows. Which is what you'll be doing anyway when the neighbours look on with a mixture of awe and envy at all your good deeds.

Modern
manners

How to turn down a big invitation

Whether the pleasure of your company is requested at a wedding, birthday or bat mitzvah, you still have free will (something that may slip your mind when overbearing relatives are involved) and you are entitled to say no.

Maybe people will be upset, maybe they'll never speak to you again, but if they love you enough to invite you, then logic dictates that they will love you whether you turn up or not. And if they don't react with at least a modicum of understanding, it means you weren't invited for you, anyway, you were invited for them.

The most gracious way to handle this is to call or send a note or email saying you can't come. (You don't have to give an excuse, but if you feel you absolutely need one, bear in mind that not being able to find a babysitter works only if you've been given less than a month's notice.) Then tell them you'd love to take them out to dinner at a time convenient for them to celebrate. Having dinner at your house does not count.

The other option is horribly underhanded and recommended only if you either (a) hold this person in quiet contempt or (b) believe them to be stupid, because it is insulting. It involves a last-minute phone call explaining that you or your significant other or both were just involved in a bingle or a brush with chickenpox and are so, so sorry but you sadly can't make it. Such a performance requires an absence of moral fibre and should ensure that you won't be invited to anything else of theirs for a very long time.

How to react to a gift you don't like

It was Jerry Seinfeld who said that if you repeat the name of the gift, you can't possibly like it. So, avoid saying something like 'Cliff Richard's greatest hits!' this Christmas – it's a dead giveaway.

This is one of the many small rules that you must observe in order to pretend you like a present. And you must pretend. Because it is only one moment in time, and not pretending may lead to well-intentioned feelings getting hurt.

The exception is if the gift is hugely expensive and comes from a loved one you are close to. For example, if said loved one buys you jewellery you don't like, you must speak up, but only privately.

Otherwise, it's business as usual. If you know a person who always gives bad gifts, you're actually in an enviable position because you won't be crushed upon unwrapping an XXL 'I heart Barcelona' T-shirt.

For anyone else you're unsure of, you can try my sister-in-law's tactic with my family: beg off, telling everyone you are too overwhelmed to unwrap any-thing now, but will open all presents later. Bless her, she gets away with it every year.

If that fails, you must feign delight. It's important that you're sober when you attempt this, as micro facial cues displaying contempt and disgust might be fleeting but will register in the gift giver's brain forever. A simple 'Aww! Thank you!' and it's done.

Just keep the gift nearby because if you kick it away or break it to fit it in your car boot, you might offend someone – but only if they see you.

Good luck.

How to properly introduce yourself or someone else

I'd like to introduce this by stating that introductions, while a seemingly perfunctory aspect of social life, still often end up a little awkward, what with all the hand shaking and the forgetting of names and the introductions that come too late. So, let's start with the easy part.

First, never leave a 'Hi' hanging, always follow with your name. It seems straightforward but it's funny how many people in the moment leave it to the other person to ask. So, begin with a 'Hi, I'm Jenny.' Save the 'Nice to meet you' for after the other person has spoken as it cannot be nice to meet them until you've, you know, properly met.

If you're at work, include your surname and your position. Or if it's the beginning of a social conversation, contextualise yourself. So, 'Hi, I'm Jenny – I'm the sister of the birthday girl' is the way to go. It's important, too, that when introducing you always state the name – either your own or someone else's – before occupation or relation.

If you're introducing one person to another, and you've contextualised them, the next step is to draw out a common interest. For example, 'Jenny, this is George. George works with the birthday girl. George, Jenny is the birthday girl's sister. George and I were just talking about how nobody reads books anymore. Jenny, you're a big reader, what do you think?' And when they're both safely ensconced in conversation you can excuse yourself.

If you're introducing one person to a group, then it's 'Jenny, this is George, Jo and Will. Everybody, meet Jenny.'

It used to be that you introduced the host or the older person first but these days it matters little.

If you've forgotten someone's name it's far better to come clean than to not introduce them at all.

Finally, if you're sitting, it's always best to stand when being introduced. It used to be that men stood for women but I think only good can come from standing up for someone, no matter who you are – it looks commanding, too. And you'll need that if some old crone pulls out the dreaded 'And you aaare?'

How to be a good neighbour

Neighbours, while appearing to live, quite literally, on the margin of your life, have the ability to make it a living hell so it's important to mind your manners – and your boundaries.

It's great if you're a social person, as communication is important – you don't want to wake up one day and have to broach that awkward sewerage situation with a stranger – but you don't need to go overboard either, so don't be nosy.

If you live in a house, mow your lawn. You'd be surprised just how much an unmowed lawn can drag down your neighbour's own property (and general mood). If you own a pet, make sure you clean up after it. If your dog barks, don't simply shrug your shoulders – that barking is annoying! So take it for walks.

Don't park in anyone's driveway except your own and make sure you tell guests where the demarcation lies.

Dispose of your garbage thoughtfully and securely – vermin and birds and other such horrible creatures can migrate all too easily.

If you're having renovations, give plenty of warning, and please, for the love of God, don't start until 8 am.

If you live in an apartment, the same rules about renos apply. Also, don't play loud music, dry your hair or turn on your washing machine after 10 pm.

If you're throwing a party, invite your neighbour along – they're more likely to feel part of it and less likely to call the cops that way. A word on that: if someone does call the cops, then TURN THE MUSIC DOWN.

While you may want the world to know what a skilful lover you are, your neighbours may find this actually kind of gross, so please, restrain yourself.

Experts recommend chatting or at least saying hello to the elders of the neighbourhood – they've usually been around the longest and have intel on everyone. Besides, they'll most likely appreciate a chat more than almost anyone else.

How to deal with passive aggression

Passive aggression is so maddening because it's often difficult to prove. 'Did that just happen?' you may ask yourself after your friend, who knows you're trying to eat well, gives you a box of chocolates. 'Was that really just a coincidence?'

It's this underhanded hostility, an ambiguous way of cutting people without having to take the blame, that can lead you to question your sanity. But can I just say: if you've been the victim of this and you're still smarting over it, remember that almost no one is innocent here – we're all passive aggressive at one time or another.

It usually takes hold when a person is discouraged from being assertive or expressing their anger. This may have started in childhood or it may be a by-product of the domineering relationships they find themselves in, where they don't feel like they can communicate openly.

Knowing all of this, you should treat the passive aggressive person with a small amount of compassion, because underneath it all they really feel like a trapped child.

But it doesn't mean that when someone is consistently late, or 'sick', or silent on the phone, or putting off what you asked them to do, like, 50 times already, you should take it lying down.

If you do confront them, old El Paso is likely to deny it or play dumb and shift the blame to you. Your best solution is to lead by example. Encourage open communication by expressing what you will and won't put up with – as it crops up. Don't bring up old grievances.

Ask them questions. 'Are you upset?' is a good place to start. It's important to ask it right after they've done something underhanded: that way you're showing them you aren't about to fall for it.

And keep it light-hearted. Feel free to laugh when repeating their excuse to them: 'Ohhh! *Of course* you were asleep at 5.30 pm when I called! How could you not be?' You'd be surprised how much tension can be dissolved with humour.

How to apologise properly

Ali MacGraw told Ryan O'Neal in *Love Story* that 'love means never having to say you're sorry' but this is patently untrue. In fact, it's our loved ones who can hurt us the most – precisely because we care so deeply about them. Having said that, an apology, delivered in a heartfelt manner, can heal in powerful ways. Just don't overuse or misuse it or you will devalue it.

But when we say it properly, sorry is often the hardest word because we have to swallow our pride to deliver it. To cushion this pride, some people use the old 'I'm sorry you were offended' line. Dear reader, this is wrong! You're still not accepting responsibility and by shifting blame onto them you're inflicting further harm.

If you've had a fight, wait until you've both calmed down. Screaming 'I'm sorry!' in the middle of an argument can, believe it or not, be interpreted as sarcastic.

Next, don't expect that by blubbing 'Sorry' everything will immediately go back to being normal. Forgiveness is one thing but, as Jonah Hill told a classmate who wet his pants in the movie *Superbad*, 'People don't forget.'

Begin by explaining what you know you did wrong without offering any excuses. Then tell the person how sorry you are. If the offended party is worth their salt they won't rub your nose in it; instead, they should accept it by saying thank you. Next, talk to them about possible ways you can avoid repeating your behaviour in the future. Then, you can finish with a hug, unless of course it's your boss or a police officer or a judge, but if it is any of the above, I'm sure an apology is only the beginning. Sorry about that.

How to politely refuse advice

It doesn't matter if you're suffering from a bad relationship, a career impasse or the common cold, there are always going to be people who believe they know what's best for you and have a firm desire to impart their advice. Why, look at me – I'm doing it in this book.

However, as a reader, you can always turn the page. Advice is harder to avoid when you're face to face. You can try the path of least resistance – a couple of quick 'Uh-huhs' and a change of subject. But if, for example, they insist 'Have some prune juice – I drank it every morning and within two weeks I was pregnant,' or offer a forceful 'Why haven't you told your boss you want a pay rise yet? It's obvious he's taking you for a ride,' it can quickly become aggravating. You can again shut them down with a shrug, but this is unlikely to help you long term.

My advice is a little nauseating but, then again, so is prune juice. See, the person is advising you (and probably many others) because what they really want to show you is how clever they are. I know this because, well, as I said, I'm doing it right now. It's not really the subject but your reaction that counts. So, nod your head slowly to convey your awe at their specialised knowledge and, as you're nodding, open your eyes wide, as if you've just seen the ghost of Aristotle, and then firmly and pleasantly reply, 'Yes! I know!'

How to behave at a funeral

This is not advice for those who have lost a loved one. There are no rules for the grief-stricken and there is no advice to be given, only comfort.

This is for the person who is attending the funeral of someone they either don't know very well or are only distantly related to. It's also for the person who attends the funeral of a loved one's loved one; you're there as a back-up – a privileged position – and it's important you rise to the occasion, no matter how sombre.

The first rule is, be on time. This isn't a wedding.

Wear conservative clothes that are black. For women, this means a blouse with pants or a knee-length skirt, or a dress. If you don't have black, navy or another dark colour is acceptable. For men, it's a suit, and, if possible, a tie. There are no exceptions to this rule. Maybe the family is reframing it as a 'celebration of life' – well, it's going to be a celebration of bogan if you wear jeans.

Don't sit down the front. The only exception to this is if you're the back-up person and your loved one wants to, but overall, it's best to make yourself as unobtrusive as possible. There will definitely be a few quiet tears, and unless the congregation all have stiff upper lips, there may be serious outbursts of emotion.

You should approach the bereaved – even if you've come alone. Offer your condolences (an 'I'm so sorry' is fine) and then quickly move on. You can linger, but only if the person you came with wants to.

Do stay around for a little while after the service. Again, if the person you're with wants to attend the wake you should join them. But if it's a person you don't really know who has passed, it's fine to go as soon as people start to leave the service.

The entire day might feel a little uncomfortable if you're not familiar with the person who died, let alone the great mark they left on the world, but don't try to overcompensate by reaching across a pew or a few people to hug a virtual stranger. People are grieving, not crazy.

Tricky
situations

How to escape a party bore

Not unlike a leech, a dull party guest can stealthily creep up, casually attach themselves and suck the very life out of you.

Personally, I am more inclined to put up with someone who talks my ear off over someone who has nothing to say, but either way, it's an altogether unpleasant situation for glitteringly charismatic people like you and me.

If it's a quiet, shy type you can't shake, the first thing you can do is ask plenty of questions. This will do one of two things: they'll respond with interesting answers and thereby solve your problem, or they'll find your interrogation technique overwhelming and make a speedy exit.

Do not hesitate to draw another person into the conversation, either. For example, 'It's so weird that you say that because my friend Gail loves early-'90s pub-rock bands as well! Gail? Did you hear that?'

But if it's a guest given to soliloquies and they simply won't be interrupted, then the only thing to do is gulp down your drink (make sure you always have one) and, as soon as they draw breath, let them know that you simply must get another.

If they insist on following you to the bar or the ice-filled bathtub, tell them you desperately need to empty your bladder. If you have to act as if you are pulling down your pants to prove this, by all means do so. It's just the sort of mildly antisocial act that's bound to send anyone running scared. Mission accomplished.

How to leave a party early

It's getting late, but the party is far from over. Or it's early, but you're tired. Or someone has just made a faux pas from which neither of you can recover tonight. It's time to go.

If you have kids, this is a no-brainer. Everyone knows you can blame them for everything. And if they're not there – so much the better. The sentence 'Thomas is flu-y' can be used to great effect.

For a small gathering, it can be as simple as going to the toilet, as this 'soft' exit will subconsciously prepare your host for the real thing. When you return you can announce how tired you are and – bam! – you're on your way.

If it's a large party, you're in a much better position. Pick a time when two or three people are leaving and piggyback onto their farewells, thereby minimising any chance of a drawn-out goodbye.

The other option involves sheer stealth and is widely considered politically incorrect: simply disappear. Begin with the fake phone call and slowly walk outdoors. Keep acting as if you're listening as you wave to other guests. Roll your eyes – anything to maintain an aura of authenticity. Then, when you're close to your getaway transport, hop in!

Be warned: this is not for the faint of heart, but if you're a love-'em-and-leave-'em type it's the perfect crime, because no one will ever really know when you left.

You can explain yourself in a polite text the next day; meanwhile, your mystery and your reputation (however uneven) remain intact.

How to react to an insult

Unless it's a no-holds-barred argument, or an episode of *The Real Housewives of New Jersey*, it's rare for anyone over the legal drinking age to openly insult another person. Instead, insults usually come in the form of digs or small put-downs or 'jokes' from which it's sometimes difficult to discern what exactly is being said ('Did he just call me stupid?'), let alone how to react.

Any insult comes from a place of fear; the other person is threatened by you on some level. If they weren't, they would be able to explain their opinion without resorting to snide remarks. This doesn't necessarily mean you're completely innocent (perhaps you insulted them first?), but it does mean you don't have to take it so personally.

When someone drops a clanger, try to resist a quick jab back. I advise this not just because you don't want to sink to their level, but also because any comeback will distract them from how rude they're being. See, if you're just as rude, it justifies their original comment. So, take a breath and say something like 'Wow.' This can be followed quickly with an identifier, such as

'That was mean!' or, if you're feeling feisty, 'What was that?' Questions are useful because they force the insulter to hear how rude they sound.

Just remember that most people don't wake up every morning planning to insult you, so if you find yourself offended by lots of people, it might be time to either re-evaluate your relationships or look in the mirror. No offence.

How to respond to a nosy question

It can be anything from the size of your mortgage repayments, to when you plan to have children, to what income tax bracket you're in. And while plenty of uninhibited people don't mind answering these sorts of questions, others find them invasive, even off-putting. What to do?

First, it helps to understand that the person asking might come over as a little nosy or tactless, but chances are they're only curious. Generally speaking, no one is trying to generate tension, unless the question is leading – as in 'When was the last time you applied deodorant?'

If you're gutsy enough to reply 'I'm not comfortable discussing that,' you probably don't need to read this. Maybe you have your own publicist? But for everyone else, the key lies in not caring about the slight pause in conversation that might follow.

Faith Salie, an American radio host, once gave this advice to those on the receiving end of a prying enquiry: 'Let the simplicity of your response be a lesson' – and I happen to love that.

So, if the question is about the price of your house, you can limit your answer to one word: 'Expensive!' Or if it concerns the timing of potential offspring you can say 'Soon!' Likewise, the answer to how much you earn can be as simple as 'Less than I would like' or, if it's obvious you are earning a motser, you can respond with 'I do okay.'

Laughter (even in the face of tension) should ensue and then, together, you and the nosy parker can swiftly jump to a new subject.

How to respond to too much information

Judging by social-networking sites, online media and the 24-hour news cycle, it seems as if we already live in a culture of too much information. There is even an acronym: TMI (as if you didn't know). When it occurs through one – or all – of the above, it's easy to turn a deaf ear or to de-friend on Facebook.

But what happens when someone spills their guts and there's nowhere to run? If it's an off-colour remark from a co-worker, for example, you are well within your rights to respond with a firm 'That is too much information' in order to shut them down. In my experience this usually works. Just don't yell 'TMI!' – unless you're younger than 15.

Similarly, if a taxi driver tells you about his wife's incontinence or a fellow sports patron complains about the after-effects of a powerful curry, you can respond in the same way, adding 'Thanks, mate' for good measure.

It can become trickier if it's your friend explaining how her birth plan went awry or your mother telling you too much about your father's bedroom preferences. At this point, it's no longer about a response but the setting of a boundary – and fairly quickly, too. I have ploughed through such inappropriateness with a yelp of disgust followed by a forceful 'Woah!'

But if the person still won't cease, you can quickly excuse yourself. If they ask where you're going, tell the truth: after listening to their over-share you're off to take a shower.

What to say in an awkward chance meeting

They can strike at any time: you're out for a walk or at the local shopping centre, successfully minding your own business, when – bam! – you see them. We're talking the casual acquaintance, whether it's a co-worker, a friend of a friend, someone from high school or your ex's mum.

You've made eye contact and now it's too late – you are going to have to say hello. If you have a dog or children or an iPod you can do the walk-hello. Do not stop, do not slow down – simply wave, say 'Hello,' point to your prop (be it pet, child or earbud), smile like you're Miss Universe and trot on by. If you feel any sort of guilt you can always text the person later, explaining that you were in a mad rush to get to the physio.

If you're someplace else where you can't easily get away – in a lift, for instance – it's time to pull out the small talk. Under no circumstances are you to attempt an in-depth conversation. But going too shallow (chatting about the weather, for example) may come across as forced. So after the initial 'How are you?' hit the flattery button. A 'You look great!' can take your run-in from awkward to relaxed in less than two seconds – provided they don't look as if they need a kidney transplant. If it's a co-worker, you can add 'I didn't recognise you out of your work clothes!'

If you haven't seen the person in a while, feel free to use that Holy Grail of compliments: 'Have you lost weight?' It's guaranteed to leave you both feeling warm and fuzzy.

What to say when you don't know what to say

I'm not talking about the moment your crush passes by and you find yourself tongue-tied. I'm talking about those times in life when something unspeakably tragic befalls a loved one, a friend or colleague and you have no idea what to say, or even if you should say anything at all.

The first rule to remember is that if you don't have an existing relationship with the person, now is not the time to cup their face in your hands and tell them how sorry you are, while making deep and prolonged eye contact.

If you do have a close relationship with them, you should first discern how guarded they are. For example, if your great-uncle Max is not given to outbursts of screaming tears, it's best to just act a little more warmly than usual and then go on pretending that nothing has occurred. But if the person is an emotional extrovert, or if they're simply open, you may approach.

If words fail you, that is precisely what you go with – 'I don't know what to say' – because in these sorts of instances gestures can be as powerful as words. The notes that read simply 'Words fail' or 'I'm sorry' are preferable to the flowery, impersonal ones – although those never hurt, either.

Just don't change your tone of voice or tilt your head when you see them because, while the person might be wounded and broken, they are still the person you know.

How to make small talk

The art of making small talk is an extremely useful skill to have, because, when you've mastered it, it enables you to turn a potentially stiff situation into a warm and cosy one.

What's more, it can take a relationship with someone you're trying to impress (a boss, an in-law, a speed date) from mediocre to memorable in minutes.

Discussing the weather or current affairs is perfectly acceptable but these topic choices can also scream 'I'm making small talk' louder than your own conversation, which can make people feel more awkward.

So, after the initial introductions or hellos, find something you both don't like and pounce on it. Research shows that nothing bonds people faster than a shared hatred of something or someone. It's important that you don't dive straight into bitching or you'll come off as a negative person, but if there is something you don't care for, don't be shy.

Next, ask the person what they think of this negative thing. Not only will they value being asked, and will therefore be more likely to open up, but it also prevents you from looking like Eeyore.

If there is absolutely nothing negative to pounce on, don't panic. I know it's tempting to talk about an area of your expertise but this can make you appear boorish so avoid it if you can. Instead, go directly to Stage 2: vulnerability. Open up about something you're unsure of at this event (not how you don't like small talk!) or something that happened to you when you felt a bit foolish – if it's funny then so much the better.

Be mindful not to overshare. For example, 'This restaurant reminds me of the one I once vomited in' is not recommended. But a self-deprecating story reassures everyone that you're only human. They'll be able either to relate or to sympathise and within minutes they should open up like a bloom in spring.

How to be silent

This is very easy if you're by yourself, isn't it?
Unless you're the type who talks to themself, which
apparently means you're smart.

But unless you're an introvert – a 'good listener' –
or you're one of those rare creatures who welcomes
silence, sitting in a quiet room with another human
being can be a frightening concept. It is simply too
tense! And so we feel compelled to rabbit on about
the weather or our unwatered plants or something
equally frivolous in order to fill the dreaded silence –
and before we know it, we've made ourselves feel
foolish. Oh! What to do?

If you're in a room with someone and you've run out
of things to say, you know what? It's actually fine!
Some of us have been raised to think that silence is
synonymous with disapproval – hence the anxiety.
But it's actually not. It's simply part of the natural
ebb and flow of life, so relax into it as you would a
warm bath.

Don't whistle, don't hum, don't even sigh – all of these
things signify nervousness and will only exacerbate
any perceived tension. Simply smile and enjoy the
quiet. It could well be that the other person needs

silence – or at least a gap in conversation – in order to gather themselves.

However, this level of equanimity might take some practice. In the meantime, if even silence in the cinema makes you nervous and you absolutely cannot take it, there are options.

If you're in a car, first aid can be found by simply switching on the radio. Do not plug in your iPod as this looks terribly antisocial.

If your introversion would put a porcupine to shame and you know you'll be in this situation ahead of time (perhaps you're a houseguest of people you don't know very well) then plan ahead and bring a book. Worst case, you could always play on your phone.

And remember, it won't last forever (even though it feels like it will).

How to handle a bad housemate

A person doesn't have to rifle through your drawers or indulge in aggressive make-out sessions on the couch or hold impromptu drum-practice sessions at 3 am to constitute a bad housemate – although the above are hardly minor misdemeanours.

Everyone has horror stories and it only takes a couple of small yet significant incidents for you to feel like you're living in a minefield, where the only safe places are your room and possibly the bathroom, but that's hardly rock solid, depending on your housemate's level of creepiness and the lock situation.

You may feel frustrated but, dear reader, do not write notes. They are terribly passive aggressive and achieve nothing, besides displaying your own unique blend of cowardice and self-righteous indignation.

I believe that if the relationship has broken down to this level, a heart-to-heart isn't going to make all that much difference. Instead, try to install small rules as you go – or, even better, draw up an agreed page of guidelines on the day of the housemate interview. And if you're the housemate, the same applies.

The key, now that your home has become radioactive, is to *treat it like it's radioactive*. Stay out a lot. And leave home early. And when you are home, stay in your room.

But of course you can't do this forever and so, depending on the lease situation, it's up to you to either move out once it's up, or have the conversation about ... how your relative from Romania that you've never mentioned until now is moving in.

There is also this: you don't have to wait until the lease is up. It is possible to break your lease. Oh, I know, the money! The money! But as anyone who has blown a wad on travel insurance will tell you, what price can you put on peace of mind?

How to respond to panhandlers

Oh goodness me, this is a hard one, isn't it? How do you know if someone is truly down and out or if they are stuck in the cycle of addiction?

On the one hand, giving a destitute person money is the easiest way to let them know they're not invisible: you see them and you're not about to step over them.

On the other hand, studies show that the loose change you're gracing their palm with won't do any good long term. It's harsh isn't it? This is because homeless people can only spend their money – they can't save it. So no matter how much money you give them, unless they have infrastructure and direction in the form of housing, a recovery program or charity sponsorship, as well as your money, it's not going to do a whole lot.

The fact is, giving money may be more about us and our need to offload our guilt than any need that the homeless person has.

But what to do?

Well, you can always give them money anyway, to show them that you know they're a person and not an inconvenience.

But if you really want to make a difference, check out your local charities who support the homeless and those who've fallen through the cracks in our society. Organisations such as the Salvation Army (salvationarmy.org.uk), Shelter (shelter.org.uk) and Centrepoint (centrepoint.co.uk) give you many different ways to contribute. You can sponsor a room in a hostel or you can just simply donate money. In these cases, every little bit helps.

Family

How to cope with challenging in-laws

In a perfect world, everyone would have Sally Field for a mother-in-law and Steve Martin for a father-in-law and you'd all join hands underneath a rainbow to sing 'Kumbaya'.

Alas, in real life certain in-laws can be a little challenging. That might be too weak a description for some but it is the most diplomatic one, which brings me to my first tip: maintain diplomacy.

See, when you entered the family unit, the dynamic shifted. The parents (and in some cases the siblings, too) are no longer Number One in your spouse's life – you are. Or you should be. For some family members this is a tough reality to accept, so if they're less than pleasant, relax and give them time.

'Talking it through' is not recommended. Nor is trying to become their best friend. If they're just not that into you then these strategies, however well meaning, will only make it worse. Instead, keep your head down, smile a lot and keep any opinions to a minimum.

But what if your mother-in-law has made a catty comment about your eating habits, or worse – your parenting style? What if dear old Dad-in-law has cracked one too many jokes that are poorly disguised insults?

Unless they are downright abusive, do not react. Reacting only inflames the situation (which can quickly devolve if that's exactly what they're after). Also, it hurts your spouse. So turn a deaf ear. I mean, literally act as if you did not hear what they said.

It's also worth mentioning that your spouse needs to back you 100 per cent. This doesn't mean they have to disown their family – or even get involved in fights – but it does mean that they should have you as their first priority. It follows, too, that your spouse should be the first person you speak to about any tension – never go directly to the in-law.

In some situations, you may have to accept that you'll never be close and that's okay – you don't have to force it. You have your own family, or friends to treat like a family, right?

Having said all of that, you still have to maintain boundaries. Don't be afraid to correct a false assumption and, if you find yourself routinely insulted at gatherings, it's perfectly okay to skip one – or 10 – depending on your level of tolerance.

How to deal with other people's misbehaving kids

I'm not talking about a Stage 5 tantrum or a screaming baby here. Such events are largely out of the parent's control and are deserving of pity rather than scorn. What I'm referring to is the tendency some littlies (and others not so little) have to run riot, either in a shop or restaurant or your own home, while their primary caregiver has the tendency to turn a blind eye.

If it's a restaurant and you can see as soon as you enter that there's a table filled with a gaggle of six-year-olds celebrating a birthday party, then ask to be seated somewhere else from the get-go. Similarly, if you're in a restaurant and a two-year-old burps in your face, the swiftest way to deal with it is to ask the waiter to move your table.

You can't re-parent anyone (including the parents) in an instant, so don't try.

If it's a shop or your own home and Mum or Dad is present, you can speak directly to them. Bear in mind that they may get defensive and even be rude themselves (the apple never falls far from the tree), so it's imperative to keep your tone light and non-accusatory. Something like 'Is it okay if Jasper uses the bathroom for that?' should suffice.

If the parent is not present, then it's best to lay down the law at the beginning. 'Hey kids, there's no jumping on furniture, no screaming and no ball games in this house, yeah?' That way there will be no shamed faces, wet eyes or broken furniture at the end.

How to handle a tantrum

According to the experts, tantrums occur between the ages of two and four years old, when a toddler can't yet properly articulate feelings like frustration and anger and can't yet differentiate between needs and wants. It's a tad difficult, however, to keep all of this in the front of one's mind when a little person is throwing themselves into a wild fit of rage in the middle of aisle seven on a busy Monday afternoon at the supermarket.

There is plenty of advice around on tantrums, including making minimal eye contact, speaking in a low and calm voice and doing your best to get you and the kid out of the public view ASAP. Again, according to the experts, it's important not to fight fire with fire by yelling or threatening. Instead, try your best to plan ahead.

If a restaurant is a habitual place of temper tantrums, talk about it beforehand, as if you were making a verbal contract. For example, 'We know that we can behave in our high-chair at restaurants, right?'

And choose your battles. If a kid wants to throw a Stage 5 over a ribbon, let her have the ribbon. However, it's best not to give in to the major stuff, like a seatbelt, if you can help it.

Encourage talking: 'I know you're angry now, so tell me, using words, what exactly the matter is.' Which, again, can be difficult if someone has dirtied their nappy in frustration.

These directions are all aimed at toddlers. If an adult in your life verbally attacks you, throws something or even raises their voice, there is only one mode of recourse: leave – immediately. Don't fight back; don't try to talk them down. Leave the room and don't return until they have calmed down. They may not know the difference between needs and wants but you sure do, right?

How to cope with a difficult sibling

Maybe you're rivals. Maybe they've always been the favourite. Maybe you're the favourite and they're jealous and every. single. time. you're at Mum and Dad's they make some churlish comment and you're off into another rage spiral.

I don't want to sound like your big sister here but they may never change. However, you can do your bit so they bother you less.

The first thing is to remember who you are. You have your own strengths, even if they're not properly valued by your family. Difficult sibling relationships are often rooted in a need to perpetuate old identities. If you're branded the scatterbrain, for example, it probably means that your sibling has a need to be seen as responsible. Why? Because they're insecure. And what is insecurity except their own fear, right? So don't take it seriously. 'You never were much good with money, were you?' can be met with a laugh and treated as the leading, fear-filled comment it is.

Maybe your parents do favour them but there are still plenty of people who love you for you, so step into today! That last part sounded like the tagline of a health retreat. Sorry. But at the very least, you can stop torturing yourself because you are reacting to a past that no longer exists. Repeat after me: 'I will not regress.'

Now, if you're the favourite it's up to you to be the bigger bloke. Oh, I know! But there are few things more effective than leading by example, so be generous where you can but mind you don't get taken advantage of. Or play the martyr. Handing out cash while rolling your eyes, for example, will only perpetuate both of your old identities.

Which now begs, if I may: Are you secretly hanging on to this old identity? Because that way, whether you're 'responsible' or 'scatterbrained', you can keep blaming and not change? Don't worry, I won't dob. Just think it over, would you?

And if it's all too much then limit your time with them. It is better to see them twice a year in a peaceful setting than see them once a week and fight like cat and dog.

How to succeed as a stepparent

It's hard enough being a parent but being a stepparent has its own unique challenges. The boundaries are murky and you may be trying to relate to someone who doesn't want a bar of you – and that's just the tip of the iceberg.

The first thing you can do is either show or tell your stepchild that you are not trying to be a replacement for their other parent. Even if the other parent is absent or abusive, you are you and you're not here to take the place of anyone else. This goes without saying if the other parent has passed away but can be just as difficult during heated custody battles, so watch yourself.

You are to have absolutely no opinion on custody battles, or anything else related to the other parent, by the way. Yes, you can support your spouse and talk about it with them but your stepchild must never ever see or hear you make a single comment about their other parent.

Next, don't try to win your stepchildren over with gifts or affection or anything else. Kids can spot neediness and insecurity a mile away because it looks incredibly dorky, so stay open and warm, let them know how much you value them, but don't pal around.

Now – and this is just as important – don't discipline them. If your spouse asks, you must politely refuse. It's difficult when you're in the heat of the moment, so if they're being aggressive or disruptive, speak to them as you would to any other person you're not related to (i.e. don't yell and don't threaten).

Finally, give them plenty of time with your spouse – alone. They may love you or they may see you as a homewrecker but either way it's very important that you give your stepchildren and your spouse time to adjust.

And be patient! Whatever turmoil you're going through, what the kid is going through is much worse, because at least you had a choice in the matter. So hang in there because change, no matter how difficult at first, will only make everyone stronger.

How to be a good godparent

Time was, you were selected for godparenting duties if you were (a) deeply religious or (b) a viable guardian replacement. In some cases, both rules still apply, but for the vast majority, godparenting is your friend's way of telling you you're their favourite, or your sibling's way of telling you they don't trust outsiders. Either way, it's a flattering gig.

First, the basics: birthday cards are mandatory, birthday presents preferred. Remember that the kid is not going to make the first move on account of the fact that they are a kid, so it's up to you to stay in touch and be consistent. Don't be one of those self-pitying types who thinks 'Oh, Lucinda probably doesn't want to hear from me,' because at least up until they enter the sullen teenage years, they're usually overjoyed to have a visitor – especially if you arrive bearing good gifts. A word on that: you can't give good gifts if you don't first get to know what they like, so put the time in.

Even if the parents are religious (and you are, too), it's still not considered polite to stick your nose in, so avoid any long sermons on the importance of prudence and sobriety, for example. What you can do is model for them what a caring, responsible adult with solid self-esteem looks like.

If you can't do that, then be the eccentric godparent and show little Lucinda what happens if you make poor life choices. There is no better advertisement for prudence and sobriety than a string of dysfunctional relationships and slurred speeches that begin with 'Don't ever fall in love, kiddo!'

How to choose a last-minute gift for your dad or your mum

We all know that, as adults, presenting our mothers with a shoebox diorama full of misshapen macaroni or our fathers with a golf ball is no longer acceptable. But there are plenty of grown-up versions of the diorama/golf ball, including the guest soap and the photo frame.

I'm not suggesting you fork out loads of cash (although perfume or fancy cologne never hurts), just be sure that the gift you choose for the person who gave you life shows at least a little bit of thought.

First, identify your parent's style. I'm not talking about whether Mum's an 'autumn' or a 'spring' on her seasonal colour chart; I'm only suggesting that you refrain from giving her the memoirs of Shane Warne – unless she also happens to be a fan of prolific spin bowlers with colourful personal lives, in which case, howzat?!

Similarly, buying Dad *War and Peace* may not be the way forward if the only book he's picked up in a year is Harry Potter.

You may gift with a voucher but only if your parent knows you work 18-hour days or have a newborn otherwise, there is really no excuse for such an impersonal gift – unless it was a specific request. On that, it's fine to go sans gift if you have a pre-existing understanding with them.

For mothers and fathers who fancy themselves food connoisseurs, there is always the booking at a fancy restaurant. For television connoisseurs, you might try a DVD box set of a favourite series. If you're stumped, flowers always go over well – just don't pick them up, still dripping, out of a bin at the servo on the way to their house.

But if you've left it too late for any of these options you can go the tried and tested booze route. High-brow parent? Red wine. Earthy parent? Slab of beer. High-flying parent? Scotch. Refined parent? Rosé or champagne. Oh, I could go on all day. Non-drinking parent? Then it's all about chocolates – fancy ones, mind you – or, in the case of my dear parents, a box of Cadbury Roses.

Just remember, any parent who tells their adult children that 'it's the thought that counts' is lying. They may even be lying to themselves, probably because it's been so long since they thought about their own needs. So invoke the spirit of Warnie and go hard or go home.

How to enjoy yourself at Christmas

Maybe your relatives are better suited to a stadium — not just because of their number, but because of their potential to brawl over football teams. And maybe you have to cook for them all. Or, maybe you have to catch a plane back to what you consider to be the backside of nowhere. Maybe you have to buy too many presents for too many ungrateful people. How then, are you supposed to enjoy Christmas? Is sweat enjoyable? Is stress? Is listening to your drunk uncle's mispronunciation of 'mastication' for the 10th time in as many years?

Well, the first thing you can do (apart from inhale and then exhale slowly) is cut back on the non-essentials. Too many presents to get? Go online. Everything is online these days, and if you get in early enough, it's cheaper as well. Too many people to cook for? Ask everyone to bring something. Flying back to the middle of nowhere? Limit your stay. Cringe-worthy relatives? Don't sit next to them.

And if you can't, then, apologies in advance, but I'm going to get all Oprah on you now and tell you that, whether you believe it or not, you have a choice.

You can do all of the above and choose not to get stressed by remembering that not all of it is your responsibility. You may think you have to do it all, but you really don't. And when you step back, you'll be surprised how, after a little while, your loved ones will step in. And if they don't, if they won't, why are you going to all this trouble anyway? To gain their approval? Well, that's not love, honey. And it sure as heck isn't goodwill to all men.

Remember: Christmas is not about martyrdom — that's Easter. Or, your children's birthdays — but we'll talk about that later.

Love & relationships

How to flirt

There are among us a quiet few who maintain they can't flirt. To them I call bulldust. For flirting is merely intensified charm, a charm reduction, if you will – to borrow a cooking term.

And it's really *not that hard*. The only danger is when people go too far and cross over into sleaze. I'm raising an eyebrow at men now but I've also seen a good many women betray their basic dignity by bringing a little too much of themselves to the party. On that note: grinding up against a stranger is not flirting.

Now, as far as you are able, stay in the moment. Listen to what the object of your desire is saying. Look at them. If you (allegedly) can't flirt, you'd be surprised at what prolonged eye contact alone can do.

Ask follow-up questions, and when you do, splash liberally with a flattering supposition. Example: 'So you've been in London 12 years now, huh? I bet a lot of people miss *you* back home!'

You may gather from the above that it's okay to go a little over the top, as it displays a knowingness that you're flirting and can help break down any resistance. Just don't go over the top about anything tawdry or you'll look desperate and sad.

Experts recommend the odd touch on the forearm, but personally, I think that unless you're on a date you should forgo it in favour of purchasing drinks, which will only aid you in your closure of the deal.

Leave the teasing and insults behind – this is not primary school, people! And no French words either, as they are – how to say? – très cheesy.

How to ask out your crush

Oh, the exquisite pain of uncertain love! Is there anything more mood-altering?

First, a word of caution: even if you're brimming with desire, avoid asking your crush out on an otherwise special day or public holiday as it will only magnify nerves and – gulp! – expectations. This goes double for Valentine's Day. It's clichéd, in that red-rose-in-a-plastic-cylinder way, yes? If you wish to declare true love on V Day, it is better if you do so anonymously.

But if it's a date you seek, again, caution should be observed, lest you run the risk of ultimate failure in the form of rejection, derision or worse: the soggy response of pity.

If you already feel a frisson between the two of you, the deftest way to approach this is to invite your paramour to a party. Not a dinner party, mind, but a place – preferably a house – crowded with just enough people and plenty of alcohol. That way you can dispense with all those formalities (and fears) usually associated with a proper date and create your own dynamic under the guise of 'Well, they said I should bring a friend!'

The party is also the modern equivalent of a horror movie at the drive-in – if your crush doesn't know anyone, they may cling to you like an overzealous koala. Ka-ching! Alternatively, they may flit about the room like a moth to several flames.

Of course, the ideal is somewhere between these two extremes, but if it's the latter, just remember that anyone who doesn't get how adorable you are isn't worth pining after anyway.

How to escape a bad date

If you haven't experienced a bad date, some might say you haven't lived, for to properly appreciate the sweetness of love it helps to have experienced the sour, doesn't it? (People who have dated psychopaths may tend to disagree.)

It could be a lack of chemistry, or something they say: 'I don't think women are very rational,' for example. It could be that you simply dislike each other close-up (not too hard after that comment, especially if it's from a woman).

So, how to leave? You can always try the pre-arranged phone call, in which a close friend rings to say that a tragedy has occurred and you must exit right away. But you have to have RADA-graduate-level acting ability to pull this off properly. And it's my belief that the faking of a tragedy may bring on a real one – but I'm superstitious about that stuff.

There is the terribly unoriginal 'I don't feel well' (made somewhat believable by the addition of 'You know what? I don't feel very well'). But the best and fairest approach, in my opinion, is to make sure the date runs short in the first place – drinks as opposed to dinner. That way, if your date is a dud, after the first drink you can go on to that next thing you said you had to go to at the beginning of the date. Which is preferable to glancing at your mobile phone all night, checking the time and wishing you were sitting opposite Jon Hamm. Or, alternatively, if you're a straight male, Jon Hamm.

How to handle a break-up

Break-ups hurt like hell and they get harder as you get older because all those expectations about a certain life you hoped to share only inflate as time goes by.

However, once the door closes, you must act with dignity and sever all ties. I mean it! Pretend you're in a witness-protection program and disappear. De-friend the ex on Facebook, too.

You can cry, you can bore friends, you can hit the bottle and then hit the repeat button on Elliott Smith's 'Everything Means Nothing to Me'. But there is a reason all the self-help books advise against any contact (especially of the physical variety). It's because it restarts your emotional clock, thereby fuelling false hope – or, as the self-helpers call it, denial. If your relationship is 'meant to be', it will benefit from the break. Remember, absence pulls forth only good memories. So give it at least two months.

And please, for the love of love: none of those emails where you say you want 'closure' when what you really want is for your ex to see how witty and wonderful your prose is and then return to you. Such emails are terribly transparent. Closure (and perspective) will come with time.

Final note: a year down the track, when you think you're fine, do not be tempted by the old 'I know who can help me work out this [insert new piece of technology], my ex!', because you are lying to your ex and yourself.

Things do get easier. Even if you don't follow a word of this advice, you'll crawl out of the woods eventually, I promise.

How to relate to your ex's friends

In the wake of any break-up there is always the division of the friends. This doesn't have to be messy – you simply see the mutual friends separately. Unless you're under 18, in which case, sometimes school sucks for a reason.

It doesn't matter if the relationship lasted for a couple of months or a couple of decades; it is imperative that you do not champion your case to their friends, or worse, try to forge a deep bond with any of them. It looks desperate and weak and we both know that sort of behaviour is typical of *other people* who shall remain nameless, not you. Besides, friends always catch on to this and you're meant to like them for them – not for revenge.

However, if you did form a deep bond with one of the ex's friends during your relationship you may proceed. It's a good idea to let the ex know this, and the sooner the better, otherwise, it can feel like a betrayal. Now, as to the interaction: you must not mention the ex at all. You may lie bleeding from grief before you meet the friend, but once you arrive, it's just you and them – not you, them and the ex – so keep it classy.

If you want to socialise openly with the ex's friends and the ex and even the ex's new love interest, go right ahead; I'm sure you've done a sterling job of informing your social circle you're totally fine about it, and chances are they'll believe you – but I don't.

How to handle a negative friend

Almost everyone knows one – the type of person who can only see a glass as half empty. Getting married? 'Organising it is such a hassle.' Overseas trip? 'Nobody speaks English!'

It's tempting to respond flippantly, but the person likely has no idea what they're saying; it's simply a habit. And underneath this unfortunate habit is probably a mixture of genuine fear and guilt. They may have grown up in an environment where they were torn down whenever they accomplished something, and so, in order to avoid this happening now, they tear down their circumstances before anyone else has a chance to do so. And they'll tear down yours in case you do the same.

While they may seem either self-pitying or downright nasty, it's really only masking a strong inner critic. Deep down, they probably feel undeserving of anything good in their lives. What they need is your compassion.

Just don't confuse compassion with pity. If you pity them, you'll puff up their sense of Sufferer's Importance and magnify the problem.

First, acknowledge their situation, then go in hard on the reframe. To the fiancé you might say 'Yeah, but she's the love of your life, right?' To the grumpy tourist, 'Who cares about the language when the scenery is so divine?'

If they remain unresponsive, you might consider seeing less of them – and when you do catch up, dropping the word 'grateful' a lot. It will rub off or alienate them – either way, it's a positive result.

How to repair a friendship gone sour

Friendships – especially close friendships – can be complicated. They're not family so they're not 'compulsory' but they're often as close as, if not closer than, family. So, when a friendship turns south, the fall-out can be terribly painful and the sense of rejection is often on par with that of a break-up.

It doesn't matter if you're right or wrong; if you want to repair the friendship, you're going to have to be the strong one and make the first move. That's tough, right? But that's life.

If your friend is not given to talking about feelings or they're particularly bruised, you can try the 'show don't tell' method. This involves going out with them in a group and letting them know you care by staying open and warm toward them until you've regained their trust. This one takes a bit of time, so if they're still snubbing you after a few weeks – or even a few months – don't give up! It is, as they say, 'a process'.

If they are 'touchy-feely' you can call them, or if that's a bit scary, you can email them. You might be angry – of course you are! That's why the friendship has gone sour! But the first email is not the place to list old hurts. It's about re-establishing the connection, so apologise for your part in the breakdown. Don't expect an apology in return – not because you won't get one, but because this expectation will colour your writing. Tell your friend you miss them and you hope you can work through it. Again, this is a process, so don't panic if they don't reply right away and don't worry if you feel anxious or awkward in your follow-up communication.

If you've sent them an email or a text or you've left a voicemail and it's been a month, you can try again. But don't approach this in anger. If you were hoping to get a deer out of the forest, how would you approach that? With patience and gentleness, yes? So put your own fury aside.

If, after a while, they still have not responded, don't pressure them – you may have to accept that they don't want to reconnect. And that's all right because when you look back on your friendship you can know you did your best.

LOVE & RELATIONSHIPS

How to be the best bridesmaid ever

Some of us are born with a talent for organisation and some of us are born with a deep love of occasion. And sometimes, God gives with both hands and grants both to the one human being. If a bride-to-be is wise, she will choose this human being as her Maid (or Matron) of Honour (MOH).

If you do not fit this description but you have been selected for the honour anyway, there are rules.

First, chant loudly and often 'It's not about me.' Maybe you'd never wear taffeta; maybe you'd eschew the stretch Hummers in lieu of a humble car; but this is not your wedding.

It is, however, your wallet. It is the opinion of experts that the MOH pays for her own outfit, whether or not she has a say in it.

The MOH also organises the hen party, the bridal shower and the wedding rehearsal. You are allowed to collaborate with the bride on these but only as far as location and invitees. Everything else – invitations, bookings and games (remember it's not about you) – are your responsibility.

Of deep importance is of course the groom's ring, which the MOH can wear on her thumb. At less traditional weddings, the MOH may be called upon to give a speech – so talk to the bride about this.

It's also your duty to cascade all information down to the other bridesmaids, from the time and date of dress fittings to the bride's mood changes.

On that note, it's important to have lollies and/or Valium on hand for the big day. Holding her train is one thing, helping her hold her peace of mind is, as I'm sure you're already aware, quite another.

Food & wine

How to get into a no-reservations restaurant

It's a terrible trend cropping up in restaurants every-where: the no-bookings policy. So how do you get a seat?

Joanna Savill, co-editor of *The Sydney Morning Herald Good Food Guide*, recommends getting in early: 'Go at 5.30 pm and put your name down ... it is boring and may mean you eat at nursery hour or get hammered while you wait in the pub nearby.' It can also work out perfectly if the restaurant has a great bar where you can wait and have some pre-dinner drinks and in some cases even a selection of tasty bar food which may mean that you stay put and never make it to a table.

According to Savill, you can book ahead at some no-bookings places, but there can be riders such as having to fork out a minimum spend for the group. And beware of the trap whereby you've been elected as the person to arrive early to nab a table only to find out that the restaurant in question won't seat you unless your whole party has arrived.

Finally, don't forget the little people. 'Be nice to the person who takes the names,' says chief food critic Larissa Dubecki. 'They have the ability to work miracles and to condemn those who are rude to a lifetime of waiting on the pavement.'

And if all else fails, both ladies agree, there's always lunch.

How to test wine

One of the loveliest aspects of fine dining is the ritual of testing the wine before you and your dinner party proceed to drink it. Not only is it good manners on the part of the restaurant, it can also, if you squint, make you feel like royalty.

But what are we really doing when we 'check the wine' and give that soft nod to the waiter? I mean, apart from feeling like the ruler of a small province. Sommelier Matt Skinner says we're searching – or sniffing, rather – for two things: cork taint and oxidation.

'At its most obvious, corked wine will have an unmistakable smell of wet cardboard and mould. Smell it once and you'll never forget it. Oxidation, on the other hand, is the effect of excessive oxygen on wine. Unlike corked wine, it's possible to see the effects of oxidation – particularly on white wine, where the liquid will turn a deep gold, almost copper, colour, while red wine will generally begin to brown. The most obvious way to spot an oxidised wine is by smell: it will have lost all that lovely fruit character, and you'll be left with a wine that resembles dry sherry or vinegar.'

The general rule is that whoever orders the wine will be required to taste it when it's presented at the table. When you're presented with it, Skinner suggests that you only need to smell it. 'If you're unsure, by all means taste the wine,' he says, 'but it's not really necessary.' If the wine's bad, speak up – but don't expect it to be exchanged just because you don't like the taste.

How to properly match wine to food

There are few things more sophisticated in this life than the ability to effortlessly pair wine with the right food. I mean, wearing a monocle without irony or pretence might be among them, but it's still tough to call.

Sommelier Matt Skinner says that if you're at a fine dining establishment then the most important thing you can do is speak to the sommelier. The second most important? Give them a budget. 'Not only does it take the pressure off your wallet,' says Matt, 'but it also allows the sommelier to focus on picking out the best wines within your price range.'

Many people wonder whether they should match the wine to the food, or is it the food to the wine? See, once you start thinking about it, it can become confusing, right? Especially if you've been drinking. 'Start with the food,' says Matt. 'Give some thought to what you're going to eat and use that as a springboard to choosing your wine.'

So, what makes a great match?

'Balance. The best food and wine matches achieve this effortlessly by knitting complementary textures and flavours within the food and wine, so that the end result sees the chosen wine almost becoming an extension of your dish.'

But – and I know this may come as an unpleasant surprise – according to Matt, 'not everything tastes better with wine and there are a number of ingredients to be wary of'. Such as? I hear you ask, removing your monocle. 'Excessive levels of sweetness, spice, salt and acidity are like a minefield for most wines, as are tricky ingredients such as artichokes, asparagus, eggs and chocolate.'

But before you throw out the champagne with the brownie, Matt has these final words to impart: 'Have fun playing around with different combinations, but never let them get in the way of simply sharing and enjoying a good meal.'

How to host the perfect dinner party

There are those natural party planners who revel in the chance to cook up multiple dishes and hook up multiple decorations while mixing multiple drinks. But for others, a dinner party, no matter how intimate, can seem a little overwhelming.

The most important thing is preparation. If you're not Gwyneth Paltrow, it's recommended that you serve a cold entree. In fact, don't even make an entree, make a collection of hors d'oeuvres. Hence, there's less cooking time and therefore less stress. And, as everyone knows, you won't enjoy the party if you're stressed. Follow this with a simple main that you know like the back of your hand, and a dessert that you can make beforehand – like a cake.

It's a good idea to hold a little dress rehearsal for your dishes two nights before, so you still have time to tweak anything that goes wrong.

Make sure you always make more than you need; that way, if you make any mistakes or anyone eats more than you expected you won't spin into a panic spiral.

In fact, if you're given to panic spirals there is nothing wrong with having the whole night catered for. Better to have pre-packaged pasta and low blood pressure than a four-course meal and a heart attack.

Dinner parties work best if there aren't too many people, so limit your invitees to five, or a couple of couples.

Make a playlist on your iPod or burn all your dinner party tunes onto one CD so you don't have to change it. Make the first few songs ambient and low-wattage tracks that everyone knows and save the dance anthems for later in the night. I know Beyoncé can be awesome while you're getting ready but if guests are greeted by a feisty command to 'put a ring on it!' they may feel like they're walking into a club – or an aggressive hen's night – neither of which are especially desirable.

Candles are wonderful – especially if they're the posh type that smell of the Hamptons – but it's best to limit these, unless you want to be cleaning up wax. Instead, opt for plain white fairy lights to hang over your shelves.

Now, to the most important part: drinks. Your guests will probably bring wine and it's polite to serve it, but if you wish to appear truly chic, begin with cocktails.

The internet abounds with recipes for simple yet tasty ones.

Finally, and this probably goes without saying, hold your soiree in summer. That way, you can get away with a maximum number of cold dishes, a more relaxed night and a greater chance that all your guests will come. There's something about winter in Australia where nobody likes to go anywhere.

Of course, if you are Gwyneth, forget I ever spoke.

How to have perfect table manners

In any given movie (or novel) with a *Pygmalion* or 'rags to riches' narrative you will find the table-manners scene. It usually forms part of a montage where the lower-class lass is being transformed into a proper lady.

And the reason the table-manners scene exists, my dear, is because it's the clearest way to display a lack of refinement. Which is why it's so important that we get it right.

Let us begin. As soon as you are seated, take your napkin and put it across your lap. The waiter may do this, so wait a beat before doing so.

If the group you're dining with numbers fewer than six you should wait until everyone has been served before starting your meal. If it's a large group, you may proceed.

If the meal is truly fancy pants, you should wipe your mouth with your napkin before you take a sip of any drink.

As to the use of cutlery, work from the outside in. So, the little fork and the little knife are for entree. Now, remember this rule: liquids on the right, solids on the left. Which means that the water glass and wine glass to your right are yours, not Mr Osborne's, while your bread plate is on your left. A word on that: don't butter your roll all at once or you'll be thought a rube. Just break a bit off and butter as you go.

When finished, place your knife and fork together on the plate but don't shroud the entire plate with your napkin. Your napkin is to be placed to the left of the plate. There now, I think you've got it!

How to send back a dish

Unless you've had your head in the fridge, you'll know that food is the new opera: a veritable performance on a plate, full of seduction and lashings of drama. And chefs are the new sopranos, which makes it all the more intimidating to send back your dish – unless you're at your local fast-food joint, in which case you should probably just readjust your expectations.

If it's a non-negotiable, in that it's cold or there's a hygiene issue or it's not what you ordered, then go right ahead. Simply call the waiter over, and quietly explain the problem. But if you ordered a soufflé and you got a chocolate praline tart, make sure you don't have chocolate on your teeth when you tell them it wasn't what you wanted.

Now, for anything else, take note from reality TV: chefs don't always like to be told they're wrong.

So, before you complain, check the menu – perhaps you missed the part where it said your beef would be served carpaccio or your sashimi would come with fresh eel? Maybe you thought your serving size would be bigger (a common mistake for anyone without an eating disorder). In these instances, it's wise to use your mouth for eating, not complaining.

Having said that, don't be intimidated by your waiter (they can smell fear). So if your steak really is under-cooked, say so. It may not be fashionable, but you're the one who has to eat it, and as long as you're polite, there is no reason for anyone to be offended.

Just don't wait until the waiter has asked at the end 'Was everything all right?' to tell them no. That line is the restaurant version of 'Does my bum look big in this?' in that it's both futile and unwise to do anything but praise what can be praised and keep the rest of your thoughts to yourself.

What to do if you don't like what you've been served

We've all been there, haven't we? Well, I have, but I'm a fussy eater. You've settled in at someone's dinner party and the main course is served. It's at this moment that you raise your napkin to your mouth, for you have just dry-retched. What. Is. This? It might be undercooked or overcooked. Then again, it might be a dish that, up until this moment, you believed should only exist alive and in a zoo.

I don't want to point fingers, but in this instance, it really is the host's fault for not first finding out the dietary requirements of their guests.

Now that the unpleasant fault-finding is behind us, I'd like to add that if the host has not enquired, it's up to you to volunteer as much information as you can about what you will and won't eat when you RSVP. It's a little precious, but it's better that they find out now rather than later what a fusspot you are.

If nobody has done any of those things, you have two options. You can say you're allergic to an ingredient in the dish. That way, it's not personal so your host won't be offended. Just make sure that you say it's the main ingredient you're allergic to or they may serve it again, just without the hive-inducing ingredient.

But if that's a little confrontational for your taste, you can go directly to option two: nibbling around the thing and rearranging enough food on your plate so you look like you at least gave it a go. If the host says something like 'Oh, you barely touched this! Was there something wrong with it?' you don't have to tell them; instead, you should pull out the old faithful 'I'm just not that hungry.' Which is fine; just watch you don't then wolf down dessert.

Bon appetit!

Travel

How to pack a suitcase

Tourists, please note: I'm referring to a holiday lasting more than two weeks. Anything shorter and you are welcome to do what I do, which is over-pack, including less-than-practical items such as a porcelain statue of a poodle 'just in case', two fur coats and a large glass bottle of perfume. For those journeying for two weeks or more, I offer the following tips.

First, look up the weather in your destination for the time of year you're going.

Take enough underwear to last you a week, making sure to stash some underwear in your carry-on bag, just in case your luggage goes AWOL.

If you're going overseas, we all know we can take on no more than 100 ml of any liquid so it's worth buying the little miniatures of toothpaste, mouth wash, etc. I find cleansing wipes and hand sanitisers to be particularly useful, especially if you're sitting next to an armrest hog.

Experts recommend taking enough clothes so that, should you wish to, you can wear a completely different outfit for five days. Although, everyone is different and some people place a low premium on clothes-washing, so by all means, go by your own instincts (provided they involve a strong instinct regarding your own body odour).

Now, for every T-shirt you have, fold it in a buttoned-up shirt and then fold the shirt around it. This prevents creasing. Nifty, right?

Take a plastic bag to put all your dirty clothes in and stash your socks in shoes to save on space. Don't be afraid of the old vacuum-sealed plastic bags, they really do help you ... find more excuses to shop.

How to observe in-flight etiquette

Travelling to Europe might be a breeze but anything further afield means more long-haul flights and several hours onboard a plane. So it's very important to mind your manners.

This might seem obvious, but make sure you hold your carry-on luggage in front of you as you walk down the aisle — you don't need to give strangers a black eye before you even start drinking. And a word on that: we all know it's not a great idea for you to imbibe heavily, but that is none of our business.

It will become our business if you start acting like you're at a game of two-up, so if you're afraid to fly, take the Valium option and skip the gin and tonics.

If you have kids, ensure you have enough things to keep them occupied. If your kid won't stop crying, try walking with them up and down the aisle. Yes, this can help to settle them, but it also gives the people closest to you a break from the screaming.

Observe personal space — use those headrests to stop yourself from snuggling into a stranger. And if no one asks you about your Life Story, do not volunteer it

– not everyone flies to make friends. Do not hog the armrests, either; this is not your lounge room.

And I know it's 7 whole hours to New York but that doesn't mean you have to keep your seat reclined all the way for all of the flight. You can try, but please understand that swift kick to your tailbone is unlikely to be accidental.

Bon voyage!

How to be a good houseguest

We all know better than to overstay our welcome or leave the bed unmade when we lodge at another's home, but there are plenty of little moments of potential awkwardness that, if not properly avoided, can add up to a terrible time – for everyone.

If you have your own room, then congratulations, you've effectively halved the awkwardness. If it's the lounge room, you know the rules – last one to bed and first one awake. Hey, if you want to sleep in, there's a hotel up the road.

I'm sure I don't have to tell you to clean the bathroom after you use it. You'd be surprised at how much hair you can leave behind in the basin alone. Oh, you think that's gross? Then you've obviously never had the type of visitor who is comfortable walking around in their underwear.

Now the little things, such as who puts away the dishes or who does the laundry, really depend on your host. Lots of people like their homes to stay a certain way, and to even suggest doing the washing up is a no-go. But you should always offer.

Take whoever lives there out for dinner at least once during your stay. This gets everyone out of the house (a welcome relief for all if it's not a mansion) and means no washing up. Be sure to either chip in for groceries or buy your own.

And buy them a thank-you gift, too. Wine, chocolates or flowers are best, but if you've been walking around in your underwear you're looking at Cristal Brut.

How to take care of a borrowed car

If you've read Voltaire or seen *Spider-Man*, you know that with great power comes great responsibility. This notion comes into crisp focus when you're behind the wheel of your brother's V8.

Of course, it doesn't have to be a V8 to get the blood pumping – the loan of someone's bike is enough to set my hands wringing in a nervous dance of unwanted accountability.

Just remember that if someone does loan you their car and their name isn't Mum or Dad, it means they trust you – so try to trust yourself too.

Before you pick up the keys, make sure you have insurance settled. They may already have it covered, but it's best to ask – especially if you're under 25.

Of course, you know better than to speed or to eat and drink in the car, to say nothing of smoking. It doesn't matter if it's a pig-sty when you pick it up: as a borrower, you're automatically held to a higher standard.

Finally, it's always a nice touch to fill the tank before you return the car. And if your mind isn't already clouded with worry after all these instructions, try to relax and remember what your loved ones will tell you should you crash it: it's just a car.

How to merge in traffic

It's an oft-repeated observation that people are getting ruder. Nowhere is this more obvious than on the road. This is, at least in part, because there are more cars (and bikes) than ever before.

Yes, there are road rules, but some road rules are not often policed – including those that govern merging.

The most annoying merging crime is also the one that's most frequently committed: the old trick of speeding, overtaking 10 cars, and then putting on your blinker in the other lane to push in. It's the worst, isn't it? And yet, who hasn't done it?

My inclination is to let the person in (what's the big deal?). But some people become crazed at the injustice of this essentially selfish move, so if traffic is particularly congested, please don't do it. Alternatively, if you do go ahead, remember what you've done the next time someone else wants in.

If it's a general merging of all cars from a motorway or from two lanes into one, you should follow the zipper rule: one car from one lane follows one car from the other. This is pretty standard so if you push in you'll almost certainly earn the ire of your fellow motorists!

Next: put on your blinkers. It seems strange but a proportion of people (usually men) don't use them. Isn't that a trip? They see it as a sign of weakness.

You know better than to speed up when you merge but it's important not to go too slow either, as this only slows down everyone behind you and stops up the flow. And as any yoga teacher will tell you, a stopped-up flow is seriously bad karma.

Finally, and probably most importantly, once you've snugly transitioned into the next lane, don't forget that most sacred of all road courtesies, which every driver appreciates: the thank-you wave.

How to handle road rage

Maybe you accidentally cut someone off. Or, perhaps it took you 20 seconds to notice that the light had turned green. Whatever it was, if you look gingerly to the right or left, you can probably see a fellow driver, gesticulating wildly with rage, staring back at you. Perhaps they've plucked a few colourful words with which to describe your driving skills – or your appearance.

Depending on the sort of person you are, this can be either terrifying or infuriating. If you're terrified, that's okay – just breathe deeply, stare blankly ahead and try to leave the scene as quickly as possible. If an apology is in order (and the person doesn't look like they're capable of violence), make a meek look with your face and mouth 'Sorry' in a desperate manner – and keep moving.

If you really don't believe you did anything wrong but the person is abusing you anyway, the same rules apply. No good can come of fighting crazy. For one thing, crazy doesn't respond rationally so your protestations are unlikely to get through to them.

If you're the sort who is easily angered, it's up to you in this moment to hang on to your temper. Nobody benefits from counter attack – this is of utmost importance if your partner and/or kids are in the car. Think about the example you're setting for your kids!

If, however, you're the one who tailgates and cuts people off and drives angrily (or, as you might describe yourself, 'someone who is sick of all the idiots on the road'), I've got news for you: it's not about the road – it's about your anger issues. You take them out on other drivers because that's when you feel powerful. But you're hurting other people, so if you don't like therapy, at least Google 'angry driving' so you can stop, revive and ... get help!

Social media
& technology

How to observe mobile phone etiquette

Mobile phones have come a long way from the old days when you had to yell into a grey plastic brick, and yet there are still some people who remain stuck in the dark ages when it comes to basic phone manners.

I mean, we all know the 'Please switch off your mobile phone' screen they show at the start of a movie is not just a suggestion, don't we? And of course that sentiment also applies to speeches and churches – especially if someone is being buried.

But what you may not know is that while you believe your conversation on the bus or in any other public place is so fascinating and funny that it's worth PERFORMING by ENUNCIATING every syllable and laughing loudly, it's actually – forgive me – obnoxious.

Equally obnoxious? Texting while someone is talking to you. This especially applies to close relatives, who seem to cop this more often than anyone else. Studies show you cannot listen and text at the same time.

Finally, and this is a personal peeve but I think it's worth raising: go easy on the text language. OMG, I dnt care hw long U'v been doing it 4, if U'v got time 2 txt, you've got time to spell it out.

I know this all seems a little harsh, but think of the phone as another person. Would you start talking to another person in the middle of a conversation? Would you talk loudly about personal problems with another person in a public space? If the answer's no, then don't do it with a phone, either.

How to respond to online gossip

A wise person once said, 'What people think of you is none of your business.' But these can be tough words to live by if what people think of you is all over certain Twitter accounts, Facebook walls or emails.

If it's in the form of bullying from other kids at school, it's a serious issue so let your parents or a trusted teacher know straight away.

If it's an incriminating photo of you, you can email the person and ask them to take it down (as politely as possible, of course).

If it's simply a mistake but one you believe will damage your reputation at work or with people you care about, you are welcome to respond. It's helpful, should you take legal action, to keep all of your responses in writing – just so long as they are utterly free of emotion. I know, it's tempting to shoot a zinger back online but, as perverse as it sounds, any reaction, in the eyes of those who thrive on gossip, is a good reaction, and it will only fan the flames – so, don't bite.

However, if you believe that what's been said is defamatory – seek legal advice. But here is where it gets tricky: the defence is often that a person's opinion is not fact and therefore difficult to prove as defamatory. If you'd still like to go ahead, make sure you hang on to all correspondence between yourself and whoever is making the claims. (This is why responding without emotion is so important – you don't want to muddy up your own case.)

I wish you all the luck in the world but urge you to remember that people are very forgetful and that this too shall pass. And while you may feel the sting for decades, everyone else will have moved on – the quicker you can do the same, the better it will be for you.

How to untag yourself from a Facebook photo

We've all been there: you receive a notification that – surprise! – you have been tagged in your best friend's brother's workmate's photo.

For the well adjusted, this missive carries only a moderate feeling of curiosity. For the rest of us, the fight or flight response kicks in and what follows is a frantic navigation of Facebook profiles followed by a manic pushing of buttons until you can look upon your identified picture. And, guess what? It appears that your half-open, bloodshot eyes, double chin and sweaty hair make somehow a less-than-flattering image. Worse, you appear to be holding aloft some sort of oversized wine glass and you're spilling it into your own lap. And that's if you're lucky.

Don't panic. First remove the tag by clicking on Report/Remove Tag under the photo which will untag you in the photo and remove it from your profile. The photo will, however, still remain on the uploader's album. What to do?

Begin by mustering all of your charm and then combine this with a hefty dose of courage. Now, craft an eloquent, overly polite email to this person, letting them know you had a great time (well, obviously, look at you!) but would it be okay by them if they removed this photo from their album? If you feel like they might put up a bit of resistance you may invoke the following terms: 'new job', 'strict work policies', 'interview coming up' and, the real heart-tugger, 'a boss who hates me'.

Finally, to guard against future embarrassment, it's possible to review posts that friends tag you in before they hit your profile (although this doesn't stop the tags appearing elsewhere). Click on Account, then Privacy Settings, then How Tags Work, and then turn Profile Review on.

How to extricate yourself from Facebook

When was it? Ahh, was it circa 2004 that you first told the world your status was 'excited!', that you were 'in a relationship' and, judging by your profile photo, also fortunate enough to be extremely photogenic? It was a simpler time.

But now, all those friends later, the enthusiasm has waned. Facebook has helped you reconnect not just with school friends and work friends but that dastardly ex and their friends and, oh dear, both your parents.

Then there's the time wasted once you're on. Oh, you tell yourself you're just going to check out your friend's birthday snaps but before you know it, you're down the wormhole and clicking on the status of your ex-lover's lover's pet Dalmatian. It has become, to borrow the parlance of the relationship option, 'complicated'.

It's time to quit – and, just like with smoking, you've got to go cold turkey. Practically speaking, you can do two things: deactivate or delete your account. The instructions to deactivate are in the Account Settings, and remember that this doesn't remove your account and you can reactivate it down the track. For those wanting no chance of getting back on the wagon, it is possible to delete your account permanently, but this is trickier and, at time of writing, it was necessary to access this through the Help Centre and then to submit a request to do so. Facebook claims that while content of deactivated accounts is saved on their database, content of deleted accounts is removed (although 'copies of some material (photos, notes, etc.) may remain in our servers for technical reasons'). Make of that what you will.

Now, how to fill the void? Well, if you're not a purist you can log onto Twitter – it's the nicotine gum of Facebook: you're still getting a hit but, without the pictures and the room for so much detail, it's not as damaging to your health. Besides, Twitter is hipper anyway.

But, if you mean to go offline and stay offline, you can always try something radical: arrange to meet up with a friend and connect – whisper it – face to face.

How to get more followers on Twitter

We live in a fast-paced world ruled by technology so I don't have time to sugar-coat this for you: Twitter, like life, is a popularity contest and she who tweets often – and with great humour – wins. Technology may have changed our world but the rules governing popularity are as old as The Hills – and I don't mean the television show (that's, like, so passé).

Begin by tweeting to those who are a step above you on the social ladder. Tell them what they just tweeted is 'ah-maze-ing!' and tweet with conviction. In other words, don't say 'ah-maze-ing'. When they tweet back, tweet again, this time adding something witty or interesting – and you will now have the attention of their followers. All going well, they'll now follow you.

You may occasionally retweet what another person has said – this is the 21st-century tribute and an inventive way to suck up. The use of hashtag (#), once employed to make searching easier, is now used to cheekily sum up your modus operandi and is the easiest way to be funny. But use sparingly – jokes still get old in the Twitterverse.

Follow everyone who follows you, unless they're a stalker. And avoid the overuse of website links – yes, they're informative, but people want to hear from you, not a URL.

Finally, avoid the 'blag' – the bland brag. Tweeting 'hubby just brought me bfast in bed. am luckiest girl in world!' is a sweet thing for your husband to read but has the opposite effect on the rest of your followers so always think before you tweet. Unless you're a celebrity and then you should tweet with abandon – we need something to entertain us in this fast-paced world.

How to observe online dating etiquette

Online dating is probably the most straightforward and efficient way to meet other singles, but that doesn't mean it is without its own rules – and snares.

Anyone who is not completely naive will understand that profile photos are a better-looking version of yourself. Just please, make sure your pic is from the last two years, not the last time you had hair.

Studies show that profile pics of people while they are out or have a drink in their hand gain more attention. I know I don't need to tell you that more skin also equals more interest – from all kinds. This can be a double-edged sword, so keep it sophisticated. And smile – this leads to more interest as well.

In your first message to someone, stay breezy and upbeat and focus on them – nobody likes a braggart.

If you've reached out to someone, allow a week for them to respond. People lead busy lives and they get nervous too, so chill out. And don't barrage them or you'll run the risk of looking creepy or insecure or both.

If someone reaches out to you and you're not interested then replying with a brief and polite 'thanks but no thanks' is, in my view, better than silence, but plenty of people stay quiet.

If you've been on a date where there were no sparks and the person contacts you again, do not disappear. This is very rude and can quickly decimate a person's self-confidence so, stay polite. A simple 'I don't think we're a match' is enough. Do not give a litany of their faults! Calling them a loser does not automatically make you a winner.

On the other hand, if you've met and had a good time, don't be offended if their profile is still up there – it can take a while to establish trust so don't demand they take it down either. People want different things, but if exclusivity is what you're looking for, it's best to wait at least three dates before you raise it. Ask them how they feel about that and go from there.

Now, I don't want to sound like your granny, but if you're a woman, always meet near your home and never late at night. Tell at least one friend what you're doing. For tips on how to handle a bad date see page 90; otherwise, remember to keep your wits about you and stay brave – the same philosophy applies whether you're online or at the bar: there is no love without risk.

Work

How to work smart not hard

If you're the sort of person who finds yourself consistently staying behind at the end of each working day while your colleagues traipse blithely out the door, or skipping lunch because you have 'too much to do' – or, that old chestnut, popping into the office on weekends – then it's time to face facts: you're working too hard.

Of course you're busy. But we live in a busy age, don't we? So how can it be fixed?

First, make sure that when you're at work, you do work! Often, we lag back at the office in the evenings or at weekends because we've spent so much time procrastinating – telling ourselves we're just going to check the weather, only to emerge half an hour later from a wormhole, with two tickets to Amsterdam and half-a-dozen luxury items added to our online cart.

Next, delegate! I know, nobody can do anything as well as you can, but they'll never improve if you don't first give them a chance. And stop telling yourself it's 'just easier' if you do it – that will bite you on the behind in the long run and might be one of the reasons you're now in this position.

Allocate a block of time when you won't answer emails or the phone to cut down on multi-tasking. An interruption – however small – takes 10 minutes to fully recover from.

And take those breaks. Even if it's a walk around the building, it will clear your head and improve your concentration – and your mood.

Put a time limit on all your meetings – this will make others more efficient too.

And, last but not least, have a conversation with yourself about why work has taken up this much room in your life. What are you avoiding? What space are you trying to fill? Work that one out and you won't need work quite so much.

How to blitz an interview

In his best-selling book on gut instinct, *Blink*, Malcolm Gladwell explained that people make up their minds about other people in the time it takes you to finish a cup of coffee.

I don't want to add to your nerves, but when you're at a job interview you've got to make those first precious moments count. Especially because the whole point of the interview is for your prospective employer to 'get a feel for you' – they've already seen your qualifications.

Do your research by finding out as much as you can about the company before the interview. Dress neatly and conservatively. The only exception to this is if it's a creative workplace, in which case, you should still dress conservatively with a modicum of flair.

Make sure you arrive 15 minutes early. As well as reducing your stress and making you appear punctual and professional, this is also psychologically valuable as it puts your potential employer on the back foot. That's ruthless, but hey, so is the interview process.

Now, I can't stress enough how important it is to have a firm handshake – especially if you're female. Too many times I've shaken hands with a small, limp mackerel masquerading as a hand and I have judged the person for it. Don't let this be you!

Should you ask questions? Definitely, but make sure that your questions are specific and that you're able to show off how much you already know about the company when you ask them.

Be prepared for questions, too, such as what your strengths are, where you'd like to be in five years and the old chestnut: what are your weaknesses? Warning: now is not the time to admit to laziness. But replying with 'I'm a workaholic' looks transparent so somewhere in the middle – that is, 'I'm a fairly critical person' – will do. And while you may be critical, bitching about your former workplace makes you look – believe it or not – bitchy, so avoid it.

You might be anxious, but don't zone out and don't try to overcompensate by being cocky. For instance, putting your feet on the desk and announcing 'Well, you can stop looking, sweetheart; the chosen one is here' can be off-putting. Especially if the recruiter is male. And smile, too.

Finally, relax. Research indicates that the majority of employers choose people like themselves — it's called unconscious bias — so if they don't like you, chances are you wouldn't want to work for them either. Good luck!

How to ask for a pay rise

Statistically speaking, women are far less likely than men to get a pay rise, for many silly sexist reasons I can't go into now, but also because they find it difficult to ask and, if knocked back, will probably never ask again. So if you're female, chances are your pay increase is long overdue.

First, make sure your side of the street is not only clean, but sparkling. Arrive early, work hard, keep your head down. It really is the little things. And, this may be slightly controversial, but it helps if you've already been taking on extra work before you ask. It's not really fair, but then neither is capitalism, right? So, load up on extra work to prove you are capable – and be consistent. I'd give it three months – you want this to look genuine.

Now, a guaranteed raise earner is of course the old 'Another company wants me' move. But you should only pull this one out if (a) it's true and (b) you've already been to the interview and talked money. If your boss values you, they'll up your salary and if they don't, well ... do you really want to keep working for someone who doesn't truly value you?

If you don't have another job up your sleeve, then your annual performance review is the best time to, uh, raise this. Compile a list of every extra thing you've been doing. Talk about your successes and, above all, remain positive. Maybe you deserved a raise last year but acting like you're entitled to it won't get you one any faster. And, no matter what, you should always give the boss a week or so to mull it over.

It may be that you get the 'We aren't giving out raises this year' or 'There is a staff freeze' response, in which case you can go to a company that wants you. Or, if it doesn't work this time but you don't want to leave, you can act like a man and keep asking.

How to get more from a business meeting

Can I flag this with you? I hate meetings. I find them tedious. But apparently meetings can do wonders for team morale; they also promote communication in the office, and increase efficiency. Who knew?

Apologies if you're already across this but according to the experts you must agree to a time limit before you begin. This minimises the tendency some people have of going off on tangents. (Another thing I'm guilty of. Sometimes I'm knee-deep in a personal anecdote when I look up and realise ... as I'm slowly realising right now ... that I'd best get back on topic.)

Next, come with an agenda – and stick to it. If you're the person conducting the meeting, it's your responsibility to gently pull everyone back to focus. Having said that, sometimes tangents can lead to breakthroughs, so it's important not to be too strict with them.

Write everyone's ideas down – there is no judgement in brainstorming! Pen and paper are also useful props if the idea is a bad one and you need somewhere else to look when you don't want to give someone a flat-out no.

If you often find that people tune out, make sure that when you wrap up the meeting, you repeat the main points. As in: 'So Ken, you'll be finding last month's figures, while David, you'll be shadowing Ken.'

Finally, email everyone with all the points covered (or if you're some fancy manager, have your PA email everyone) and, as you've just drilled down during face time, go easy on the jargon or you may find that the benchmark you've set will not be properly actioned by your team.

How to recover from an email faux pas

It was Monica Lewinsky who warned that there is no such thing as a permanently deleted email. A sobering thought if you've ever sent an email in which you complain about the boss to the boss, or an email intended for your loved one to a co-worker.

First, breathe. Everyone makes mistakes and every reasonable person knows this. The next thing to do is pick up the phone and apologise. You can make a joke if it's appropriate, but don't make any excuses.

If you're simply too mortified to speak, you can quickly send another apologetic email but a phone call allows the offended party to see you for what you are – a feeble human being groping for mercy – and this can only help your case.

If you've made a typo, don't worry about it, you can let it go. In fact, if it's a small error you can look slightly neurotic if you send a follow-up email explaining it. If you accidentally hit Reply All, then just hit Reply All again and say sorry. No big deal. Same goes for CC'ing.

The only email faux pas you really have to watch out for is the flaming missive, where you finally give that person you loathe a piece of your mind. This isn't so much a faux pas as an anger management issue, so before you hit Send, save the message in your Drafts folder and sleep on it. Then, the next day you can delete it. Although, if Monica is to be believed ...

How to deal with a loud co-worker

Okay, full disclosure: I am that loud co-worker in the open-plan office and if you cut me I will bleed (that is, if I'm not too busy chatting my head off to notice), so please be gentle.

And I speak from experience when I recommend first checking your motivations before delivering that shush. In fact, it's best never to shush (unless you work in a library). But if you're tempted to tell that co-worker to pipe down because they're discussing a topic you're not interested in or not familiar with, take a moment and ask yourself: Is it really about the noise? Or is it the fact that you're left out of the conversation?

However, even I'll admit it can be annoying when a person won't shut their trap – especially if it's affecting their (and your) work.

As with any problem, it's best to knock it on the head straight away – do not let your resentment build up, or you'll soon be known as the noisy one. Politely ask the chatterbox if they wouldn't mind 'keeping it down' as you've got a terrible deadline – that way your request is about you, not them, so any hurt feelings are minimised.

If it's someone from a different department, talk to their boss. If you are their boss, do not attempt to solve the problem by sending an email giving them an urgent task to do. Not only is this passive aggressive, it also shows you're afraid to tackle issues head on – not great leadership material.

If they still won't tone it down, you can do what I do when someone manages to make more noise than me – surreptitiously pop in your iPod earbuds.

How to give negative feedback

It's easy to whinge, whine or sigh loudly if you're displeased with a co-worker, a spouse or your own kin. But it's generally considered more effective if you explain clearly exactly what the problem is — preferably straight away.

Before you begin, remember that as long as you deliver it with kindness, you're only going to help this person by providing them with this feedback. And if they don't take it well, then you've learnt something about them, so it's really a win-win scenario.

One traditional method involves the old positive-negative-positive sandwich. Often disparagingly termed the 'crap sambo', it still gets my vote as the most helpful and straightforward way.

First, open with the fluffy good news. If it's a co-worker or subordinate, begin by telling them what you love about their effort. If it's a friend or a spouse, tell them what you love about them.

Then, proceed to the filling (the negative part, the crap) by prefacing it with something that shows you're empathetic to their mistake or weakness.

For example, 'I know you've been strapped for cash but deodorant is unfortunately not an optional extra in this office.' Or, 'I know you honestly don't see the dirt, but you've left shoe marks all over the carpet.'

Then, close with another light comment to show that while you may not care for what they've done, you still care. Follow up with a specific solution and garnish with lots of kindness. Before you know it, they've swallowed the sambo – crap and all.

How to disagree with your boss

The positive-negative-positive technique (see page 161) also applies when talking to your boss, with one important exception: as George Clooney told Brad Pitt in *Ocean's Eleven*, 'The house always wins.' (Unless your boss has a combative nature and enjoys a bit of argy-bargy, in which case go nuts!)

For most of us, though, it's best to accept the final outcome, even if you don't like it. Alternatively, you can find another job. I know it can be tedious, especially if your superior has selective hearing, but there are ways to work around it.

Begin by agreeing with the general sentiment of what your boss is saying: 'Yes, you're right, we do need greater productivity.' Follow this with the golden rule of subordinates: before you criticise, come up with a better plan, and gingerly, too, so as not to appear disrespectful or negative.

If your boss gives you a flat-out no, it is reasonable to ask why (a good boss will always give you an explanation). You can also present evidence of why their idea may not work, but again, make sure your approach is deferential.

All of this might seem timid, but it's easier to push your views if your boss already feels that you're on their side. The use of 'we' instead of 'I' also helps to convey this. As in, 'Can we really do that when so many of us are already working overtime?'

Now try saying it without the tone, Missy, and you'll be fine.

How to respond to radio silence

So, you've sent off your CV or your big pitch or your proposal for a rooftop garden on top of your work building, and while you're trying not to slip into a pond of paranoia and despair, it feels like it's been a while now and still ... no response.

Should you wait it out? Lie low? What happens if you confront? Won't that feel like you're nagging them?

Well, if you know that this person is habitually late with everything or a known procrastinator, you can step out of the pond. But that does not necessarily mean you have to sit idly by your Inbox.

The best solution to any problem always involves prevention. So, it's a good idea to make sure that you leave a deadline at the end of your email. For a CV, that can be a little uppity, but for everything else you can close with 'If you could get back to me before October 21, that would be great.' That way, when you 'check in' or 'touch base' just to see if there has been any news, you won't have to feel intrusive. Besides which, a deadline is helpful for the receiver too as it helps them prioritise.

If it is a CV or something of a sensitive nature, the standard waiting time is a week. After a week you may begin to craft your email. Just make sure you're polite, humble and, above all, enthusiastic. For some employers persistence is a virtue – and one that can make all the difference. Especially if they're indecisive or lazy or both.

Dear Reader,

Well, here you are at the end of this marginally-bigger-than-your-pocket life guide. I hope you feel a little wiser, a little stronger and a little savvier about navigating some of the hairpin turns that can make life challenging on a day-to-day basis.

So much of what we call etiquette can at times appear awfully twee. But good manners are really nothing more than guidelines for how to live your life with others in mind – how to work through situations without causing anxiety or hurt. And 'self-help' is really nothing more than understanding pain and hopefully lessening it. If we think about the greatest advice we can remember, we may also remember it involved easing such pain – both for others and ourselves.

With this in mind I'd like to leave you with one final piece of advice, which is that no matter how many rules or guidelines there are, you can never really follow them all. And you shouldn't try to – perfectionism is very boring and *faux pas* are part of life. Besides, if everyone adhered to the rules we'd have no one to gossip about. And where is the fun in that? In the end, none of us is perfect (not even me, dear reader) and, to borrow a line from one of my earlier entries if I may – and I think I will: *that's okay too.*